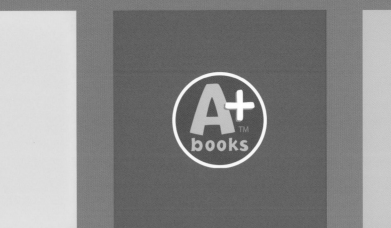

Shapes around Town

Squares

around Town

by Nathan Olson

Capstone
press

A+ Books are published by Capstone Press,
151 Good Counsel Drive, P.O. Box 669, Mankato, Minnesota 56002.
www.capstonepress.com

1 2 3 4 5 6 11 10 09 08 07 06

Library of Congress Cataloging-in-Publication Data
Olson, Nathan.
    Squares around town / by Nathan Olson.
    p. cm.—(A+ books. Shapes around town)
    Summary: "Simple text, photographs, and illustrations help readers identify squares that can be found
in a city"—Provided by publisher.
    Includes bibliographical references and index.
    ISBN-13: 978-0-7368-6371-1 (hardcover)
    ISBN-10: 0-7368-6371-0 (hardcover)
    1. Square—Juvenile literature. 2. Shapes—Juvenile literature. I. Title. II. Series.
QA482.O47 2007
516'.154—dc22   2005035855

Credits

Jenny Marks, editor; Kia Adams, designer; Renée Doyle, illustrator; Kelly Garvin,
    photo researcher/photo editor

Photo Credits

Corbis/Alan Schein Photography, 14; Farrell Grehan, 4–5; José Fuste Raga, 11; Mark E. Gibson, 7;
    Owen Franken, 12; Reuters/Alessandro Bianchi, 18; Richard Hamilton Smith, 22–23; Royalty-Free,
    21; Ted Horowitz, 6; zefa/Alan Schein, 16; zefa/Erik P., 10; zefa/José Fuste Raga, cover;
    zefa/K. Solveig, 13
Getty Images Inc./The Image Bank/Grant Faint, 24–25; The Image Bank/Pete Turner, 19;
    Photographer's Choice/David Madison, 20
Image Farm Inc., 17, 26–27
Shutterstock/Martin Green, 8; Riddle Photography, 9; Robert Zehner, 15

Note to Parents, Teachers, and Librarians

The Shapes around Town set uses color photographs and a nonfiction format to introduce readers to
the shapes around them. *Squares around Town* is designed to be read aloud to a pre-reader, or to be
read independently by an early reader. Images and activities help early readers and listeners perceive
and recognize shapes. The book encourages further learning by including the following sections: Table
of Contents, Which Are Squares?, Welcome to Square Town, Glossary, Read More, Internet Sites, and
Index. Early readers may need assistance using these features.

Table of Contents

Squares are shapes with four corners and four sides that are exactly the same size. Let's look for squares around town.

Every square has four equal sides
and four corners.

Squares are different from rectangles. Rectangles have two long sides and two short sides.

Building Squares

This apartment building has shapes with four equal sides. How many squares can you find?

Squares form the windows
and walls of this curvy building.

Trees grow right in the center of these sidewalk squares. See if you can spot any other squares nearby.

Sometimes you can see
squares inside of squares.

Crisscross iron bars make
sturdy squares.

Spring brings lots of rain showers.
Rain water drains down the square
holes in sidewalk grates.

Squares in Signs

TAXI STAND

Taxi cabs and their signs are checkered with rows of tiny black and white squares.

This square crosswalk sign shows walkers when it's safe to cross the street.

NO STANDING
6 AM – 6 PM
SUNDAY
EXCEPT
FARMERS MARKET
←
SP-7098   DEPT. OF TRANSPORTATION

DON'T LITTER
8:30–9 AM
EXCEPT
SUNDAY
←

2   HOUR PARKING
9 AM – 7 PM
INCLUDING SUNDAY
←

15

Traffic signs tell us where cars can and can't go. How many of these signs are squares?

16

This square road construction sign means "watch for workers and be ready to stop."

A square hole lets workers go
below the street to make repairs.

Squeaky clean panes of square
glass frame the city sights.

Ready, set, go! Black and white
squares on checkered flags
signal the end of a race.

Have tons of fun with four squares, four players, and a ball. Can you guess what this game is called? Four Square!

What's square about a rollercoaster ride? Boards cross one another to make many squares.

Take a look around your town.
You never know where you might
find a square!

Which Are Squares?

Squares are flat shapes with four equal sides. Which of these signs are squares?

Square Town is full of square shapes both big and small. Where do you see squares?

Glossary

checkered (CHEK-urhd)—a pattern of alternating black and white squares

crisscross (KRISS-krawss)—a pattern of lines that cross one another like a grid

crosswalk (KRAWSS-wawk)—a place where walkers can safely cross the street

equal (EE-kwuhl)—the same as something else in size, value, or amount

grate (GRAYT)—a grid of metal bars that lets water pass through

pane (PAYNE)—a sheet of glass or plastic in a window

rectangle (REK-tang-guhl)—a shape with two long sides, two short sides, and four corners

road construction (ROHD kuhn-STRUHKT-shun)—to make or repair a street or road

taxi cab (TAK-see KAB)—a car with a driver whom you pay to take you where you want to go

Read More

Burke, Jennifer S. *Squares*. City Shapes. New York: Children's Press, 2000.

Leake, Diyan. *Squares*. Finding Shapes. Chicago: Raintree, 2006.

Schuette, Sarah L. *Squares*. Shapes. Mankato, Minn.: Capstone Press, 2003.

Internet Sites

FactHound offers a safe, fun way to find Internet sites related to this book. All of the sites on FactHound have been researched by our staff.

Here's how:

1. Go to *www.facthound.com*
2. Select your grade level.
3. Type in this book ID **0736863710** for age-appropriate sites. You may also browse subjects by clicking on the letters, or by clicking on pictures and words.
4. Click on the **Fetch It** button.

FactHound will fetch the best sites for you!

Index